LOVE GOSPEL BE THY, QUEEN

SHANAYA STEPHENS

COPYRIGHTS AND DISCLAIMER

Happy Reading.

Love gospel be thy, Queen

This one's for you Sharmila. Happy birthday big-sis!

ACKNOWLEDGMENTS

This book is what it is because of...

My mom and dad for always believing in me and never giving up on me. I love you.

My siblings- Sharmila and Noor, this time to help me find happiness when everything feels messed up.

Rounak Kayal and Nandini Rathore for being supportive, kind and extremely loving mentors. Forever in debt for your kindness.

My favorites and two of the best people(and awesome authors) I have ever met on Instagram -

Rathnakumar Raghunath sir and Sarika Patkotwar ma'am.

Thank you for being so supportive, kind and ever awesome.

Love gospel be thy, Queen

Couldn't be more grateful to have met you.

The inspiration behind this book -

Mom and Sharmila for being the Queens I had the privilege to cry, laugh and smile with.

The first transgender photojournalist: Zoya Lobo,

The simply gorgeous and flamboyant transgender artist I know about- Rani KoHe-nur(Sushant Divgikar) and

My favorite poet of all times Andrea Gibson who taught me love can be melting and the idea of women growing beard is entertaining!

Foreword

Dear readers,

Before we start, let me get one thing straight, I am straight. But we must acknowledge the fact that a lot of people aren't and it is not a problem.

In the recent years, with the advent of social media and 'woke' culture, mankind is on a path of acceptance and understanding. However, the LGBTQ+ community, deserves more than what they are given. This book was written with an aim of highlighting how similar we all are irrespective of sexualities we identify ourselves with. Inspired from three great persons belonging to LGBTQ+ community- Andrea Gibson, Zoya Thomas Lobo and Rani Ko-He Nur aka Sushant Digvikar, I hope this book compels you to stay silent for a while and think- "How different can humans actually be!"

In the later part of book, I have tried to pay a tribute to all women in general and celebrate the spirit of womanhood.

Happy reading.

Regards and love,
Shanaya Stephens

Love gospel be thy, Queen

TABLE OF CONTENTS

Queer

I t doesn't matter how we love and what we love...If it does, then maybe we don't understand love, at all!

Love gospel be thy, Queen

Souls of color

How do they paint our figures?

Do they see us as goofed up

Fusions of vehemence

Against the backdrop of canvas?

And maybe they paint

The passion instilled in us

With shades of red?

Maybe, the pink spreads lushfully

For all the love that beats in our hearts,

And blue for sorrows of ours

Often overlooked by souls not different from
our own,

Maybe, the orange flows with every stroke

For the hope it carries

And raylets of light in

The beam of yellow

Waiting to lighten up the walls

In the glow of equity.

The grace in our souls

Might be a halo in the art,

And the strength in our arms

Shall be the silhouette.

The pride often the

Highlighted tones in the croma,

While our cries lay in the background

Of the battle scenes

Painted in our honor,

And while there are screams

That yelp for rights

To breathe like every other being

With our heads held high,

The art is a conglomerate

Of our pains entwined with

Love gospel be thy, Queen

The promises of

Commanders-in-chief who seldom stop by.

The portraits of our kinds

Lay in colors

Of sacrifices, love, and hope,

Reuniting in our hearts

And teary in vision

We are just souls

Colorful; we don't complain

About the alien, we are perceived.

For the incompetence world carries

In knowing how diversity

Is all in perception,

But when we bleed

It's all in red.

The black and white

Suffices not what our soul

Prays for,

We love in colors

And painted in its vibrance,

See love for

What it is,

And what it could be,

Though we may not conceive scions,

Love ought to be enough

To save our weeps for sins greater than

Not abiding by the stereotypes believed.

Do they see us as colored figurines

Gleaming in joy,

Or estranged beings hung on the hope of
love,

Isolated, condemned, and broken?

Love gospel be thy, Queen

Monochromate

Right into the elixir

Life pours onto me

Envious they say words derogatory

I feel none befitting me.

My heart burps when it tastes love,

Overwhelming it's been a while,

Since I am understood for what I am.

Monochromate

They can't take the rainbows,

Say the colors hurt their black and white.

Monochromate

They don't need no shades

Stereotypes suffice.

Monochromate

I ask them why not a lil' blue, black or pink

Black and white they scream back,

Monochromate

Been a while and I ask them if it's gonna change?

Delusional, despicable, rebel, a rulebreaker,

Monochromate

They talk so loud

Kill my pride

It makes me laugh!

Monochromate

They live under a rock

And civilized though

Hate it when we talk about 'woke'.

Monochromate

They sing too aloud

And all the lyrics' whimsy,

Love gospel be thy, Queen

Equality is what they talk about.

Monochromate

Can see through lies,

Monochromate

They love teary eyes,

Monochromate

Been so long,

Monochromate, they seldom care.

Monochromate

Beauty is tagged with pronouns,

Monochromate

No religion they preach about

Monochromate

They have their own hatred

Laid down in walls

In name of one who sent his only son for our
sake.

Monochromate

Hate the way love lives

Monochromate

They preach sugar-coated childish fantasies.

Monochromate

Adventures they despise

Monochromate

All they approve gives them power to rise.

Gay

Solemnly stupid it seems sometimes

To straight people with twisted thoughts
about life,

Sin they declare it with a haughty might

To kiss a guy and being a guy?

I wonder if they make

Roses regret for praising others of their kind,

And no petal different from theirs,

Knowing each other in equal grace.

Willfully they surrender to each other's
presence,

Maybe their acquaintance with each other

As descendants of the same kind

Makes love a lot easier to be conveyed
among the fragrant few.

Or maybe they cage earthworms

Someplace in Earth's crevice,

For being with someone who knows

How to make love to them,

Trust me there's a reason

They proudly call themselves
hermaphrodite,

And still go in search of partners,

To gossip, binge or stay with at night?

Wonder how sometimes we can all be
whole,

And still a part of us will make us feel we
are in our halves?

Is it too wrong to seek our wholes

In people, who feel the way we do?

I saw no God complain,

No sky exclaim

Love gospel be thy, Queen

No land retort

No holy gospel claim

That love can only happen

When differences are not to be entertained.

So I ask the ones

That walk among us,

How wrong could it be to love?

When at the end of the day,

Together in joy we thrive.

Sometimes it may seem solemnly stupid

For straight people with hazy thoughts on
life,

To judge a guy for kissing a guy

But questions of mine seek answers from
them.

If there's all but a way to punish

A selfless devotion,

A moment of love,

An embodiment of passion

Then maybe love is stupid...

Stupid is as stupid does,

There's no reason why it should not be welcomed by!

Such a drag

Rattled in my own shades,

I paint my fingernails blue

And a French pedicure that feels so right,

When I know I am just rocking in my shoes.

Hair tied high, a crazy bun size

Bigger than egos and greater than

White collar highs,

I dress top to bottom,

In prettiest robes

The world could ever offer.

A glittered loin scissored and sewn into

My darling gown

With elegance it is brewed

In the heat of design,

And I parade in its beauty down the town
hall,

Two blocks far from where the signals turn
red.

Crimson my lipsticks

Two shades darker than the night sky fills

My lips parted to say Ciao,

And I go down, down and down the road,

Watching the crowd glancing at my
glamorous Jimmy Choos.

They whisper in my incognizance,

And the words find a way back

To my dress and

Like price tags they hang on to it.

Mean they decipher,

And sometimes of awe,

Questions linger unanswered in rows.

Love gospel be thy, Queen

Jargon, you see!

Some kid whispered back there

And I turned for a moment only to watch by
and

Smiled through my amber tinted eyes.

You're beautiful

I hear only for my smile

To grow wider and wider.

It's a drag!

Someone cheers and hell yeah!

Screams my heart aloud,

In grace I walk,

My pride intact and the street is no more
silent

When I clap.

In the corner I spot

Some hate enslaved man,

Disgust marks his wrinkles,

And his fingers entwine with some lady

Whose fashion sense I admire.

She smiles, he doesn't,

And I know for some people

It's such a drag

To make them understand

That being a drag

Is beautiful in its own aspect.

I kissed the boy

Last night, the moon felt paler

Than it was allowed to be

And the air forgot its way out from the oak it
usually visited

All these nights and the other nights

Somehow the sky knew that it was awaiting
a rain to be poured down

On souls waiting to be liberated from their
own lies

And the lies that were pressed into chests
and meant to be buried

So no one weighs them over judgmental
comments

That spread like fires down the street where
we live,

And the fear that comes with the thought
itself whistling away

With the rustling leaves,

Shanaya Stephens

I felt my heart tugging up my sleeve

Waiting to be tied down to the boy next door

Who was there waiting for me!

He was here after all this time and I saw him
once for

All he was and not too different from a
voice like mine

He seemed like a newly sprung rose in June

Lest all love poems be written in his praise

He fits not the description of the Princes
they make in fairytales

For ours was not a tele-novela love story,

Ours was a love-war, a scatheful battle, an
endless moment of toil

Because in this story the Prince awaited no
Princess that he'd help put her slipper on,

We were just two boys waiting

Love gospel be thy, Queen

To be put together as a whole.

All of the stars he'd carry in his eyes and

Still rest his eyes on my sky to be
illuminated with

The light he landed and yet too modest he
said

His world glows when I shine,

So I press my lips against his hard pressed
ones

With his stubble a little rough against my
love

As it is planted wet on his freckled face and
his eyes closed as if

Too lost in admiring the holy dream we
were living,

Convinced me that we were not ready to be
leaving,

Yet-

The world we lived for saw no flaw in the
raw vulnerability

We had exposed it to,

Funny that this world had no one but us,

The sky, the stars, the mountains nearby,

The rain that drenched our sorrows dry

And our house - the one we had shaped with
newly formed bruises all night!

Love gospel be thy, Queen

How I learnt to love myself!

The day I met myself

Was the same day I had questioned love for
what it was,

A succumbing pillar of truth held on to the
tiled marble

By what seemed like whips of neediness,
passion and garnished lies

White lies precisely,

Clinging too tight to it

That it's walls had chipped of the paint

Both of us were to trying to paint it with.

I was afraid that I might get lost

In the dark that love was

Until the day I finally find a part of me

As dark as love itself

And the hunger that it harbored for all things
insane

Made my existence more bared to me.

Of all the people I thought who had known
me better,

I was so wronged about my own self

Till the day I met love.

This body I carried craved more and more

For things people wrote only in novels

But then there was a deeper call of

A sense of gratification for things

As simple as you bringing me peanut butter
sandwiches,

Getting my hair done and a long shower in a
summer evening,

While I would sing myself electric

And Madonna would be a long lost friend

In the hymns that sounded like a virgin.

I would not seek restlessness and burnout

Love gospel be thy, Queen

To compensate for the storms growing crazy
in my head

Neither curse my ailing heart

For all the things it did to drive my brain
mad,

Criticism was a door knob away from me

Only this time I realized that it will not only
make me

But seal me up with bits

And the voids I had were merely hollows I
had forgotten to fill myself with,

The shelves a pretty empty and then

There were a lot of things to be decorated in
them

Concern in a purple band, the love for bi-
cycling wrapped in grey,

The orange wrapped love for my poems and

Red for all things dirty and mad.

The day I met myself

I knew that the people around me

Will love me if I change,

But deep in my bones all I knew that

If I was loved I would change.

So I started loving myself for

Others to love me

And the dark grew fainter, insignificant and
blithe to me.

Addicted to the eternal cascade of my
thousand sins,

I had learnt to let go of the pillar we both
had tried to hold

In a place meant to be left barren.

So I let go of all of it,

And found love inside me for what I am.

As everything came crashing down I held on
to my heart for I know,

For people to love me

Someone should love me

And only I can make it happen.

Love gospel be thy, Queen

So I did,

Choosing myself over everything

Every day, for people to like me better for
who I am, what I am, how I am,

I loved myself.

Reflections

In differences, there are thoughts. In thoughts, there are truths. In truths, there are perspectives. In perspectives there are reflections...of us and the world around us.

Escape

What do escapes look like?

Ain't it too stereotypical to be

A golden gate, lavish and grand

Leading to a secret garden,

Or maybe the rabbit hole

Alice fell down to,

And for my own pity self

Maybe it is your heart,

And if not in so many poetic realisms

All I crave is to sit by your side

And chatter my worries away,

Because all the words that are buried in my throat

Are choking, hurting

Hurting so bad

That it is felt so deep in my core and

My shaking arms as they move to embrace you

Fitting you like a glove as if they were made for you.

And that is exactly why,

I need to be out

In a happy place nearby yours,

And call out

With two open arms

Into the sky

For love to come

Howling back at me,

Like my neighbor's dog does

Every time he recognizes my fragrance each time my bike enters the lane,

In the familiar street that has housed my tripping and leaps, marathons and sweating all alike,

And that my dear is how I would like for

Love gospel be thy, Queen

Love to recognize me...

As a trespasser

So frequent in its lanes

That my whole existence becomes a second
nature

To its mighty self

And maybe the sniffs it takes

Before breaking another heart might as well
end with my standing presence.

Roaring, singing and whining at my worries

A little drunk on my wobbly feet

That dare to stand stiff in front of Cupid's
arrows,

I want to clutch love at its arms

Like I would hug

A long lost friend

Back from the school days,

And perhaps Love may not embrace me
right back,

Giving that look that we often give to
strangers

Who had walked past the road too many
times and yet

Too awkward to overlook them in crowds of
gazillion others,

Not too friendly at first

Walking on its toes,

The jolly love, walking on its toes!

Trying to make acquaintances with my tipsy
eyes and quaky shoulders

I would wait to tell love my name!

In sign languages I would give it all that it
needs to know,

For I know that we for sure don't speak the
same tongues

And that is why the few many times

I called on it; it never came,

And only the lack of words could justify its
negligence to me,

Semiotics might be our thing

Love gospel be thy, Queen

Right from the start, only that Love waited
for me

To know it quite right till that moment!

Late in life when I am too old to speak in
words again

And wise as the old oak that creaks only
when two hearts kiss,

I will pray love to transit from the escape I
have found in your heart to the

Safe heaven your arms had been to me,

I would make love stay longer and longer

As everyday it will come up with long list of
excuses

I will take Love for outings or on

Coffee dates or perhaps I will just

By the windowsill to watch Love walk out
as

I entrust it with my dreams of my gentleman

I will wake up to for rest of my mornings

And the nights I will sleep to,

But in the moment I beg you to not

Take my escape away as I see Love hanging
close to your heart

Making its way to mine.

Sometimes escapes can be people,

People who can be called ours through tests
of time.

Love gospel be thy, Queen

One time discount

To everyone who has feared to be in love
with themselves,

It's high time that we realize,

That life is a onetime discount

On your favorite dress.

You can sweat it out

With a call for a few bills to be made later in
that week,

Or pick it, tuck it, buy it, get it packed,

Wear it, flaunt it,

Make love with it,

Call it a princely reward,

And hang on to it as long as you can!

The bills and taxes

And the promises you have kept,

To be the perfect one for all

And to not spent too much for yourself

Need not be a redundant for your love of the
dress,

But not only will it push you harder to
pursue your goals,

It will also ignite the dull-dim lights you
have accolade your mind with!

Running, fighting, crying bitter,

Tossing, turning, jumping, leaning,

Holding on to it by a thread,

You will evolve for you want to wear

That pretty dress in the best way you can,

And exchange rings with fate

To show them that if there's joy out there,

Then merry is all you want to be!

Your needs are not some obligatory
negligence,

Love gospel be thy, Queen

There's no way why you shouldn't be your
priority

You have earned a million happy days

Only too afraid to work through it.

Happiness you see

Is not devoid of a price tag

And you have not only paid it in full,

But might also get

A casket full of surprises

To fill in the cracks and seal up your
sorrows.

Life is a onetime discount

On the prettiest dress, you have ever seen,

You might just go and grab it,

Or let the weathers

Weary it down as it lays unappreciated

In someone else's rusty closet!

(The offer's a bit too tempting,

To be laid untouched by other hands,

Hurry! The joy outruns even before the

Sale ends!)

Love gospel be thy, Queen

Chatterbox

Often I hear the people around me complain,

That I chit-chat a lot,

And they say that I am but a walking talk
show,

And to do away with my small talks!

From philosophical interviews

On a sidewalk,

To gossips of the day

With acquaintances of mine,

They have known me for some years now.

We talk about all the things

Big and small,

About the moments of joy

And sometimes

About the unfair games, we have for-seen,

Mostly about the future

The fate unarmed

Which we haven't called upon yet to worry
about.

Numerous rendezvous is set up

Over the little store around the corner,

And they sell not two cups of coffee for a
few pennies

But a lifetime of memories

Reinstated in talks that spill

With the warmth of the drinks.

Some days

When I feel my quiet

Has occupied the air,

I look forward to hearing from them,

And have their equal share

To let me in their secrets

From the world, they have kept so long,

No, I am not in the least bit nosy

Just been curious all along.

Love gospel be thy, Queen

Often I know that the words they speak

Are calculated at long and far

And they tell me only what I ought to hear

Hiding the truth I may need to know

And maybe the said fear

It accompanies along!

So I hear them present the fabricated reality.

At the whim of the moment

With more sipped coffee,

And they say that they mean the world to me

And I nod for there is no second thought on that

What a beautiful lie it could be!

I often say 'I love you s' for the sake of it,

Not implying in the least bit

For love to exist between two people

Shanaya Stephens

I need to know them beyond their glittery
masks,

And when they hesitate to be themselves,

It's the lack of trust I fear!

What to say when I leave,

My talky-talky tales of turmoil,

With the bills and the tip and the empty cup,

On the mahogany

Plastered with my double standards.

I hear the words corner

In a silent whisper,

New faces take my seat,

And joke on my existence

When I make it across the street,

Endless talks on the way I tell my heart out
to strangers,

Folly of mine

A guilty pleasure

Love gospel be thy, Queen

They laugh at my idiocy,

Gullible ain't she!

They laugh heartily and adjust their lipsticks
in vanity.

The cue is certain

For you to know

That all the truths in our endless
conversations

Are about to be brewed,

In front of people,

I barely know

But have heard a lot of,

In one of my little talk shows.

Another day I tip in my heels for a date,

To the same corner store,

My tongue whipped with cream and sugar,

To spread against the bitter coffee and
terrible lies,

For the audience waiting on me.

My chatterbox soul,

On a troll for being an oddball,

My audience knows me well enough and for
a long,

Yet we have rarely shook hands

Once in this brief rendezvous,

The waiter comes in and with a blink of an
eye,

We exchange the solitary truths

In between the lies I told!

I tell them how much they mean to me,

Probably lasso the moon

Or treat them with a cappuccino for the time
being,

To make them realize

Love gospel be thy, Queen

I am not talking so soon.

One of them says

What being a bitch is,

And how harsh it is often to be so cruel and mean,

I nod and smile

And slip aside from my side

On the mention of such talks!

Shanaya Stephens

The worlds around me

I am afraid that I will soon run out of worlds
to call my own

That I have started building so many tiny
worlds around me,

Surprisingly the worlds I create aren't the
ones

Where they call me God,

In one of them I am playing the part they
give to the postman

All day I carry letters in there,

From this end to that end

From one future to another

My existence is embedded in telling all my
becoming selves

Of what else they can do to not screw
themselves up

All the while in terror of unknown surprises,

I deliver them pieces of themselves and
empathize in their miseries

Love gospel be thy, Queen

Seldom do they share how lonely they think

They'll be in their prospective futures and I
tell them not be afraid

For I will be paddling into their worlds

All the while

To let them know that they can't miss out
much on life

If they don't start living at all!

In another world of mine

They call me Madman

It's funny they don't see me dressed up in
lousy trousers and colored caps but khaki
pants

And blue tinted shirts with yellow buttons

The kids there say how much they enjoy my
promise

But their mothers tell them to be weary of
me

They see a rebel in my deeds of innocence

Like that one time I told those little angels to
not wait for growing old

To get what they want

I inspired them to pursue the wild when they
were too young in the bones

Until one of them happened to believe in the
efficacy of my words

Climbed all the way up the hills and snapped

The sunset with the yellow ball going down
the crest

And beautiful it was

All the dreams in exchange for a bruise his
knee

Had added to one more of his accolades.

In another world of mine

They call me traitor and I don't mind it

I carry the title with pride as much as there's
a pretty delight

To be called out for deeds and reality checks
served to us

Love gospel be thy, Queen

In place of hardy breads and I never for once
asked them, why?

They say I had traded their dreams for
moments of joy

I retort not to their claims nor settle with
them

Instead I weigh their possibilities against my
own conscience and

I know they aren't far from truth neither
close

Just somewhere in between.

Traitor is not a word, or for that matter an
adjective

They make it apparently a state of being,

The dreams I had sold for happiness in
exchange of a tear,

But then those dreams were not mine and it
didn't hurt

To smile for some time.

I have been a traitor all the times when I
feared to be wronged

For all the worlds I have been creating
around me and

The day I forgot the one that created me,

Too afraid of running out of the world that
belonged to me,

I lay listless in all the worlds around me.

Hurting

Hurting someone is hard

Something which most people don't agree
on!

A thing or two and maybe half a dozen
tantrums thrown

Is what it takes to get a rise from the people
you have known.

So you give it a try,

You lay your plan step by step,

You turn one page

And it reads- Hard to enter, don't know
much about it.

So you turn another one entitled-

Basics of being this human,

And line by line you traverse.

You stop on the third paragraph,

Where all the great part starts.

Oh,this person cried on the first day they
went school

So did I, how familiar!

Then there's their obsession about peanut
butter,

And you remember how crazy you were for
chocolate spreads all the while in mid high

And later in life too,

That gets you into nostalgia.

Now you feel what the person could feel
about peanut butters

And you are almost thinking about giving it
another try,

Just maybe you like it when it is eaten a
special way

With all fingers laced into taste

Like you did it with the chocolate spread

Back in good old days.

The fourth paragraph is where

You learn about how much healing

It has taken for that person to be what they
are.

You read it with utmost patience,

Love gospel be thy, Queen

For to know what can break a person

You have to know

What made it stronger?

Because-"A thing is as strong as its weak
point"

You had heard it quite a few times

The day you went for movie at neighbors
and till date

You forgot the name of the movie star.

The healing began and deciphers into

Being kind.

Thoughtfulness acquires greater part of your
head,

The plan almost forgotten,

By the time you realize

How similar the two of you are

It almost breaks your heart

To break someone's.

So you stop,

And you delay all your plans,

You cancel the derogatory deeds and instead

Hop on a journey with another perspective

About life, about peanut butters and
everything in between.

You smile a lot more these days

Some people say it looks like you're in love,

And you deny it.

How can that be?

You think you have just started with life,

It seems kinda fun

All the while.

How happy and happy everyday gets,

Brand new start for the direst of things.

You see how hard it is to hurt someone?

You go deep,

Then you say you are afraid to drown,

So you try your best

Love gospel be thy, Queen

To float in the feeling

Of just being and letting it be

Whatever it is, however it maybe,

That's life,

You preach and pray all along.

Shanaya Stephens

When I am done with myself

I want to be held

On days when I am melting

With hands that have known my being

As a second nature to them.

When I am all but bared down,

Devoid of masks

Nothing but vulnerable

And breaking...

Breaking myself into shards

That hopes to pierce through truths

For it's only been so long

That I couldn't take it anymore.

On days my life seems to have no control,

I would appreciate

To be led on and to be made to hear

An 80's pop song whispering to me

That nothing can go wrong

Love gospel be thy, Queen

If all but void existed,

For things to get ruined someplace in time,

A bit of beauty they had nested,

And I would like to believe in it

With all little faith I shall have.

On days I feel like not praying

Not waiting to be rescued by God,

I would love to be accessed by kins

In simple ways

For starters talking for hours

About how much right rather than how
many wrong,

Apologizing and embracing

Everything that happened from the start, the
end

And the middle.

I would love to be accepted

For being a mess

Than losing myself with nothing at all,

When pain is the only thing that could strike
me hard

I would wait for love

To fall on me like a downpour

That had been weighing for so long on the
clouds.

On days when I am caged in my own shell

I would like to be found.

On days when there's no oxytocin in my
system,

I will wait to be revived by hugs and kisses
alike,

Bring them in and bring them all

For on the days I will be struggling to
survive

I want to learn to live...

Live so long

Love gospel be thy, Queen

For you to know that

Tomorrows become yesterdays

Not so long,

And to make it through them

I have been counting on you all along!

I want to be called

By you every moment hence

That's the only way I have believed

To go miles and miles in the ocean

Scary and deep,

Floating along the horizon I reach out for
your hand

And girl you come along every time I do

So remember, that on days when I am done

You'll let me impersonate

What you are,

Hope, deal?

Shanaya Stephens

The mornings I rise

I wake up on mornings when the sun seems
too shy

To come out of the blazing walls the sky
looks like

And the yellow spreads against the blue,

Like my own pain burning in the fierce
fumes

It hurts this time and every other time

And when it does it makes its presence felt
deep in my core.

Seeping into my bones it goes on and on

Till it finds my quivering heart

Aching and bared, waiting

To be torn down into miniscule pieces.

I pray and pray for everything in it to go
unannounced and ignored

Like the chirping canaries in the back of the
sleeping neighborhood

But like all my prayers this one too goes
unnoticed.

Love gospel be thy, Queen

The pain sees me lying listless on the tardy
couch

And the fiery tingles of its existence touches
my skin in an illusionary kiss.

Like all forms of affection that pain inflicts
upon me

I measure the familiarities and the known
anomalies that come with it.

How often it is that fear becomes

A reflection of our bared thoughts and

Why must it be the core cause of everything

Beautiful and dangerous; we have dared of
dreaming?

The thought clutches me by my collar and

Kicking through the quilt down the other
side

Of the hell my bed has been for a while,

I see it catching onto me.

The fear, the pain

I see through it

And scrounging, wailing, huffing with no
one to hear my cries

Still I rise from where I have been hurt the
most,

And watch the blazing miseries in the eye.

My heart beats through its blues

The red my blood has always been

Still warm against my skin,

The day, the world will always be a
battlefield alike

But they don't teach us to go down without
taking a bullet;

Where I come from,

And so I try to get on to my two feet

Wobbly I fall down with my broken chin,

Pain ostracized in my soul

Will it be enough to break all the dreams

Comfort has been creating in the back of my
head?

Love gospel be thy, Queen

I hope not.

Catacombs break open two blocks from
where I stand,

And I call out to those who have gone by

For inspiration and through their flimsy eyes
and free spirits they walk across

My unkempt, shabby garden and a bouquet
of half dead roses greets them

While my eyes exchanges with them the
moist gestures of longings,

In the bedlam of nostalgic embraces with
acquaintances that have already walked by

I search for my place and they nod in denial

And say it's not the time yet

Out they point to the horizon on the faraway
end

And a blithe spot of sun climbs the sky

Smile, they urge me through their halo
figurines

And paint courage into my soul where the blue lines end

Smothering beauty my heart hangs onto morphed pieces

The ashes and drift them in a brand new style.

Fragile and rejuvenated they rise with phoenix's flair.

I recount my weakness and the numerous times I have

Found my strength in the direst of times and fancy all the lies

I had almost convinced myself

To believe in about mornings when the sun never rise.

For every second I have tried to give up on life

Hope has filled me up with reasons not to comply by!

Endless I see how the dead do me favors to let me live

Love gospel be thy, Queen

The dreams they had dropped by.

So I wake up on mornings when the sun
seems too shy

To come out of the blazing fire the sky looks
like,

And I sit by my windows with my eyes a bit
wide

The air felt deep in my lungs

My fragile heart hanging on my chest

Beating through its worries of making
through another moment,

Convincing through my soulful enclosures
to the companion

Pain has been all this while

And afraid I am all the more reason

To go and try and live

For I know another moment and the sun will
show up

In the aloof sky,

And I rise from my standing place as the
morning sets up bright.

Queens

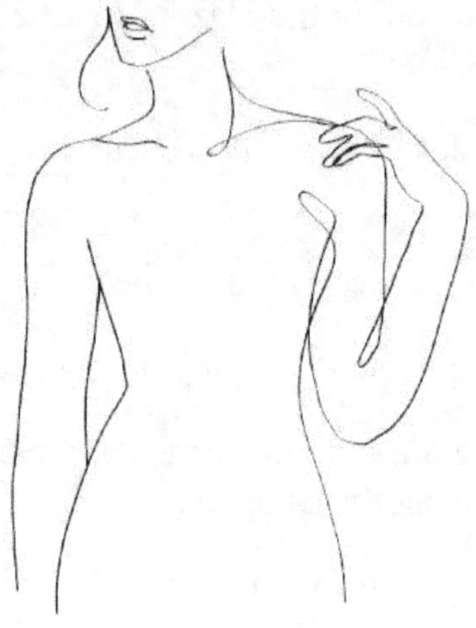

No matter how much we deny, some royals wear no crowns...Just humility, love and way too much kindness.

Boobcage

The very first time,

When I was about fourteen and felt my chest

Shaped into

Two bulged balls

Dropping down from my front,

Like loosely hung sacs,

Left to line dry in the heat,

I could never understand,

The way nature wanted my heart

To beat through

Those dangling balls,

I'd find it awkward and

To know

That one day

These inanimate

Utterly busty balls of fat,

Will feed one soul

To grow up into

A beautiful human,

Who's going to change the world,

Kept me awake

Most of the nights.

I'd sit and complain,

About how no Johns or Olivers,

Or Adams or Martins in my class,

Have to go through

The awkward misery,

When my mom had brought in

The cruelest of fabric ever made

For man-kind.

The Bra,

A cupped fabric

Shelving two spheres,

A sweet little bow

Love gospel be thy, Queen

To where the curves separated,

A pretty boob cage,

For the busty prisoners!

Lacy, silky, cottony, velvety,

Strapped, bare necked, push-uped,

These boob cages

Come in all shapes and sizes.

Why must I wear

My front in these cages?

The question lingered in my head,

A bit less long than it should have.

The Marthas, Oprahs, Priyas and Kamlas,

And their daughters and their daughters,

Had worn these cages,

Every day to the battlefield

That their life was,

And maybe in the deepest part of my
conscience,

I had made myself known,

That the boob cages

Are parts of the legacy,

That the woman in me carries

And making peace with it

Carried the souvenir

Underneath the curtain of garments,

Breathing with my chest,

The boob cage

An inseparable part of my identity.

Ten years later,

To my first encounter with the boob cage,

I un-strap it every night,

And trace the faint marks,

Left behind

Love gospel be thy, Queen

And the tight black spots

My breasts into,

And the endless times

They have struggled underneath,

To flow in the space left to them,

No constriction holding them behind.

The boob cage rests,

In my palm,

And in itself, it narrates

A story of a girl,

A woman, and this world,

She has outrun,

Conquered and seen it all,

The boob cage is a part of her journey,

From the days of abstained freedom,

To the limits, she put forth for herself,

Amidst the endless territories,

She had conquered.

Shanaya Stephens

Arm candy

Come and go as you may please,

I will still greet you with a charged smile

Laughing from ear to ear I will

Still, be the same person waiting at the
counter

For you to make it safely to the elevator

I will see you turn by as the metal gates
open wide

And swallow you whole in its mouth

Beep it escalates up in the sky and halts

Floors above where I wish to have a place to
call mine.

The distance between us stays a thick
thirteen feet wide.

You like an angel made to stay

In heavens, you have curated for yourself,

With demigods, you have brought to life

Love gospel be thy, Queen

With the stark of your pennies and your
worldly charms.

There's something about money

A lot of people say all in the world

Can be bought with a few shingles thrown
the right way,

Like tooth fairies that wait whole night

To give you a cupcake resting someplace
near your pillows,

But with money, you can not only savor the
taste of sugary cream

But make a thousand fairies flutter their
wings

As long as you want them to be,

Days and nights

Won't be the barriers to your pleasures,

Paradise is your keen place to be.

But then you think you can buy hearts too,

Benjamin Franklin, Gandhi or Jinnah doesn't
comply

With prices that are paid only in true shares
of faith,

I don't blame you for that

You've just been that way for a long way,

So maybe playing hooked

Is all that love could ever feel like

To you and that makes me wonder

If your paradise feels sore in its core

For all the bizarre beliefs you have been
paintings its wall with?

And your bedroom sheets do they ever
complain,

Or maybe you're just used to changing them

Like you change most other things in your
life.

The other day winds brushed past our ears

Too close to hear each other's whispers and
when I agreed

To show you parts of mine that I

Tag with the premium collection, lovers
only tag,

Love gospel be thy, Queen

A folly had subdued right in my head,

What could go wrong?

If for once the Prince Charming comes
along!

Everything, oh everything my dear.

You weighed the prices

To be put on around me

Shiny coat, new boots, that perfect jaw line,

Clean shaved and that black tie,

And you bow and tell me things

I don't want to believe in

We dine in some restaurant where the food
is all

but fine dined delicacy with no trace of my
home,

I wanted to leave so bad and yet I stayed.

Where are my manners!

Might I add what followed without

Our will, crippled us in the three by four
booth we have been hanging in,

Consent was stifling between us

And like every dark thing that comes with it,

I could sense a wolf howl in my head

Have fun while we can?

Nope, I said and retired for the night

Back to my duty in your apartment that
night.

You bade no farewell distaste

Guarded your lips and the wine hung on to it

Only to make it a lot savory.

The next morning

Wingman greeted me and asked

About the night and I told him the bit he was
dying to hear,

It was just a friendly dinner!

And you walk out of the elevator

A little lady goddess by your side,

Love gospel be thy, Queen

She looked wild and beautiful alike,

Blonde hair plump on her forehead short and

Deeper than blood her lipstick astound,

And she left in her little black dress and you
followed

Your paradise back to where you were.

So come and go as you please,

I will still be the person

Who greets you with a smile

Charged and laughing ear to ear,

Till there's nothing left but a year

For your heartless deeds bounty,

And the trade you have mistaken love to be
for long.

Your hundredth first mistress

Still walking down the aisle,

And I coy pretense

Just playing along.

You're too human to be not forgiven,

I chant and repeat in my head!

Love gospel be thy, Queen

Pretty is an idea!

On days I don't feel I am pretty,

I paint myself white;

Chalk powdered with compact

Contouring my flaws all blurring into my facade,

It looks so perfect and that's why

I know it's not me,

But I pretend to be perfect because I just want to be,

My skin a hard plastered smooth on my cheeks.

My dimples don't look the same

Not anymore as I used to adore them.

My lashes fall down

Coherent to my beliefs

So I paint them darker and curl them better

Wavy, lush and sleek with elegance

'If we are going down,

We'd better do with grace'

I tell them almost brainwashing myself,

Two strokes more of eye shadow

As if all the shade life's throwing on my dreams

Ain't enough to char my hope,

It burns where it is all black

But I let it be

For the last boy who'd say I look pretty

Told me they looked pretty that way,

I let them be as for him

And all the other people who think alike

Letting them engulf

My ugly in their fiery misery.

My cheeks roughed crimson

Love gospel be thy, Queen

As if all the embarrassments my scars had caused

Wasn't enough to turn them red?

How's it that my Colors were only blue and black

When red pulsated hot in my veins?

Lip tint, all glossy goes on my lips,

Stars embedded shine on all the lies that they conceal,

My fingers slide the tube a bit low and there it goes

Ruining all my pretty turmoil with a blow.

The red hue with its vermillion mess leaves behind a trail

And the mirror tells me otherwise

Of the flawed decor that garnished it,

So I stop myself and adore how raw it looks where it goes,

And let the trail follow

Up my cheeks,

On caked walls of lies

I draw Butterflies with red lines of truth

The lies agonize in the blunder

And fathom it to stop on account of their
pretentious view,

On days I don't feel I am pretty

I rewrite all the definitions of pretty out
there,

Pretty is an idea

And ideas can change

All the time, everywhere as long as you
want them to,

No more makeovers

I tell myself and my truth glares

Red and proud from the mirror,

To the last boy who'd tell me I looked pretty

I would love to hear acceptance

Come as fluently as the unwanted praises
do,

Only once for I know

Love gospel be thy, Queen

Truth comes hard way but a long way
through!

Shanaya Stephens

Mothers out there…

All the mothers out there

There's just so much that you can do

So please take a pause and maybe take a
vacation

Stay the night out at Bahamas,

Because it's only too long since the last time

You had got to enjoy a sunset by the beach

Drink from your glass of Bloody Mary and
not pretend that you hate it,

Sure you hate straw hats

So stop wearing them already

And maybe this time let no man come and
tell you

That you have a bad hair day they can make
well for you,

Giving, giving and giving so much of you

And yet you find things to give the next day

Love gospel be thy, Queen

Where are all these treasures you've been
hiding, honey?

I saw you cry alone at night

Too selfish to not come and ask

But then you don't like to be nagged at

Enjoying your own presence,

A word with yourself and what good will

I do there when all you have to is hear from
yourself!

You started small waiting to be married to a
prince

Now you run your own empire everyday

A twenty four seven

Three six five and your bouts of selflessness

That has overdone the radar all these times,

Take a moment and let people figure things
on their own

You have done so much already to call them
out on crazy mistakes

They are not too keen on correcting!

No Prince that came your way was enough
to make you feel like you deserve the world

That's because you often can't see how much
of the world

You carry with yourself when you walk,
smile, sit and laugh

There's joy when you sweat hard

And pleasure when you do it for strangers
and acquaintances alike.

You stay there silently

With a thousand words muddling up your
head

Not another devil telling you to stay back

Sure it's nowhere safe out there,

But you made heaven bow down to your
kids

Cradling them in your lap

Love gospel be thy, Queen

Singing them angels and offering them
nectar,

And what greater act of might is there

To endure all that pain between your thighs
and still be able to smile

At the byproduct of your turmoil,

'Mine!' you announce it to the world,

In pain you take your pride,

But that's just more than enough so why do
you expect to

Die for them when you have done nothing
but

Live for them all along.

Give yourself a break,

All the mothers out there,

The world's in so much debt for all the love
you have bestowed it with

Not enough to payback in seven lifetimes!

Women-you're tired

It's hard to go on

When the truth is known

But then does she ever allow herself to stop
ever

For what the heart wants?

And in this lifetime they say it's to live for
others,

It goes and gets as it catches up with time

And time waits for none

However despaired seems the day to be,

She waits on the dusks with melodious
sunsets,

Playing on the flute of a soul's merry

Too indifferent from hers,

It makes itself heard when she least expects
it,

Love gospel be thy, Queen

She craves it just too shy to admit.

Broken in ways not knowing

How many dreams have stifled and died
between her sleeps,

Sleepwalking in nightmares

Dizzy it seems often times when

Hallucinations are the sole truths fading

From realisms dense into her irises

Made to believe things she can't get and yet

Instigated to run behind them

Till she catches fire and in its flames

She burns and turns into ashes.

Too many words and too little Quense

All the things they have been preaching to
her,

Feeding her head with lies,

Happiness is a lifetime away it seems

But then she dared buying it for a buck

Back in Fifth Street under smelly beer mugs,
cakes of makeup and red tints

Painted against her drenched lips.

Pleasure is a sublimating entity

Vanishing and sour it leaves her,

None when it is needed and in gallons it
flows,

She sees when it kills her

As it goes between her legs and treated like
a luxury

She can't afford to be

Blissful and envious,

A happy woman she knows she won't be
tomorrow.

Love gospel be thy, Queen

Riveting in her chest

Beats a bird with its wings and tired it is

For being silenced and sucked into silences,

But she gives it no rest

No truths are enough for her to stop

And once she has set off

It's either do or die

So she races till the end and pays no heed.

Often things seem like they have lost their
meanings

In delusional fantasism she seeks meanings

That exists in her head half of the time,

Woman you are too tired to be

The golden trophy they cherish you to be.

She is not drunk with five dry martinis,

Just an afraid woman,

For being held behind barriers and made to
call it home

To put up with half lives and live it in
wholes,

In diasporas she lives life

And the joy they claim to be hers

When none has spared her way

None but giving and giving everything

Till she has got none to give

And perishes down as she goes,

Lightening and catching fire

So they can make an ideal woman out of her

As they carve emblems of her sacrifices,

For leaving them with all when they have
left nothing for her.

Love gospel be thy, Queen

*Women you are just too tired to be shouting
truths in faces of patriarchs.*

Brave

How is it that you often find beginnings too
scary to start on journeys

You always wished to walk through and to
give up on ideas

Way before they are born?

Slowly, steadily, fumbling and tumbling

You try and reach the start line

Embossed with our own blood, sweat and
loss and

Adamant you are that it's always gonna be
so tough and that's the way it is so supposed
to be for the longest time.

A shaky feeling snarling down the graceful
bent of your neck,

Like a slithering snake breathing heavy
against your own will to succumb

A part of your arms brazen against them and
swallow it in the whole of the peacock that
your persistence looks like,

Almost ready to give up on the smallest
obstacle in your path

Love gospel be thy, Queen

You tempted yourself to go a little too long,

But just how far?

Your conscience questions you and you
have no answers,

No one does.

As if all the bravery you were born with has
phased into a miracle of past,

You're still questioning your choices.

You see, the redundant in your journeys,
your ghostly pasts

Living rent free in your head, bringing
paying guests all the whole time- sorrows,
depression, stress, anxiety...what else?

No one to confront them

No one for the sake of losing everything,

When there's nothing and nothing at all!

Midway, you go, huffing and puffing,

Your breath caught up in our throats,

Shanaya Stephens

Too tired your heart

Oh dear! You dump in the baggage,

Just enough of everything...You know you
can't carry so much

Even if you wished to as you cross so many
worlds till you reach your own.

Its okay, you're brave,

Brave enough to ditch all the cowardice
back there

Even when no one's gonna pat your back.

Love gospel be thy, Queen

Ignorant to your own magic

You serve the charm with an ignominious flair

And see smiles curve, asking for nothing in return.

You don't dress in silk robes all days

No corset you wear too tight to robe you off all things feminine,

No man out there enough to praise you for all things wonder God have made,

Yet you think you ain't worth it,

Turn your head silly and open your arms

For if you don't know

The world is a heaven all because of you,

Embrace it, tell it out

Love gospel be thy, Queen

Joy is your crown!

Shy of all the things you done

Outdone yourselves in all things fun,

Lightening up dark places with your halo

And breaking down barriers- mean and
shallow,

No cage enough to captivate you,

No courage enough to withstand you,

No fierce like the fury of your will,

So open your eyes silly and flaunt it all,

For if you don't know

The world's a paradise because of you,

Remember it, tell it loud

Love gospel be thy, Queen

Bravery is your crown!

Cruel to your kindness

Undermining your own pretty self

Hating your body for things that lie next to
lies,

Love gospel be thy, Queen

No beauty like your name,

No art like you,

No temple enough to worship all of you,

So open your heart silly and let it all endorse
you in,

The world's a better place because of you

Hearts like yours need all the love,

Tell it loud, please do,

Love gospel be thy, Queen,

Kindness is your crown.

About the book

Love gospel be thy, Queen is a collection of 20 poems celebrating the spirit of LGBTQ+ community and the powerhouse that women are!

A three part poetry collection- Queer, Reflections and Queen.

'Queer' aims to give an insight in the life of LGBTQ+ people- the stigmas surrounding them,the opinions people hold against them and their spirit of love.

'Reflections' talk about the society and thoughts and highlights the singularity of being a human irrespective of the gender identity.

'Queens' celebrates women and their contributions to society and brings forth the joy,misery and love of being a woman.

Love gospel be thy, Queen

Other Works

Vagabond

While different perspectives amount to different conclusions, they pretty much end up in the search of peace. Peace is variable for many. This book, a collection of 30 poems; aims to take the reader on a journey, with the thoughts of a Vagabond. Hanging around the corner are thoughts of a life-loving, nomad and you, a traveler might find parts that resonate with you.

Love gospel be thy, Queen